Mail Money Secrets

"How to Make Millions in Direct Mail Marketing"

Table of Contents

MAIL MONEY SECRETS BOOK

MAIL MONEY SECRETS INCOME STREAMS

MAIL MONEY SECRETS FULFILLMENT

Introduction

Congratulations!

By reading and implementing what you learn in this book, your entire life is going to change.

This book contains the knowledge of testing, failing…and then WINNING in direct mail marketing. The secrets of direct mail marketing are in this easy-to-read book.

Before you read on though you should know.

95% of people in the direct mail industry will NEVER learn all of the strategies taught in this book.

95% of people in the direct mail industry will just keep doing the same things that FAIL over and over again in direct mail marketing.

>   (I used to be one of these people)

95% of people in the direct mail industry will continue to go to a job they hate for the next 10-40 years and never live the life of their dreams.

Only 5% of people in the entire direct mail industry will get a chance to read this book and take the advice, implement the strategies, to make a 6 or 7 figure income in direct mail marketing.

Will you be one of the 5%?

Chapter 1

Spend Money To Make Money

Chapter 1: Spend Money to Make Money

Employees go to work for a paycheck and trade time for money.

Business owners invest money in their businesses and marketing to make money.

In my Mail Money Secrets program, you will learn about how to properly invest in your own direct mail marketing business to <u>multiply your money fast</u>.

You've made the smart investment in the Mail Money Secrets program to get the secrets that you need to succeed. And trust me, this is one step a lot of people don't ever bother taking. They just keep buying into mail order "deals" without ever learning what it really takes to succeed.

You are 50% of the way there. You purchased this program. But you can't make money by only doing the first 50%! The other 50% is done by implementing the system for yourself at the end of this book in the "Income Streams" section of this system.

The income streams are the fully automated part of this business that allows you to start getting cash mailed directly to you. It's the exciting part.

It's hard to describe the feeling of waking up in the morning and feeling like every day is Christmas morning. Excited to start each day by checking your mailbox for cash.

Once you start experiencing cash in your mailbox on a daily basis, you'll never again work all day long at a job you hate. Trust me…it's just not worth it.

<u>WARNING!</u> It's true that many people lose money in direct mail marketing for years because they never learn the "behind the scenes" secrets of direct mail marketing. You will never again lose money if you follow the advice in this direct mail marketing playbook.

Making millions in direct mail marketing is simple math. Yes, what you learned in Grade 4 math is going to help you to make millions of dollars. But don't worry, there are no difficult equations and nothing that a calculator can't figure out for you.

Here's what you need to know about starting and running a direct mail marketing business. And by the way, everything in the Mail Money Secrets system is already 100% set up for you. You will just need to plug in to this franchise-like automated system.

To get going, there are 2 things that you will want to invest your money in.

1. Setting Up Income Stream #2
2. Postcard Mailings

Making the initial investment to set yourself up in the program is as important as doing the actual mailings. You'll want to qualify for the top cash payments in the program as quickly as you possibly can.

People that underestimate the importance of this in this industry tend to be the same people that waste thousands of dollars and decades trying to make something work…and never seem to get anywhere. It's okay to be skeptical, but if you trust me, you'll quickly see that what I'm telling you is only the honest truth.

I want you to succeed at this. I want you to become obscenely wealthy. My success is partly dependent on how well you do and how much money you make. And if you don't mind, once you start making money, I would like to call you so that you can tell me about it. Fair enough?

So, you can either spend a bit of money today to get set up properly in a program that really works. Or you can spend no money – but YEARS of time trying to figure it out and do something else on your own. It's really your choice.

Next, once you are fully set up, you'll want to start doing some mailings.

I always recommend you get started mailing with a BANG! In order to get your direct mail marketing business going, you should try to spend as much as you can afford off the start. Direct mail marketing is the type of business that goes faster and grows quicker with a bit of momentum to get things really growing. The bigger you can make your first few mailings the better.

I remember when I first started in direct mail marketing, I used to send out 50 or 100 pieces of mail and wait 4-5 weeks to see what happened with it. Then, I would feel disappointed that I didn't get rich, so I'd join a different program and do the same thing.

Direct mail marketing is a simple game of math. The more pieces of mail or postcards that you send out…the more will come back. Especially when you are using postcards like the Mail Money Secrets ones that have already been tested and proven to convert into sales.

It's easy to blame program and system owners for your lack of success in direct mail marketing. I used to do that too. But when I learned the real secrets about how to actually make money in this industry, that's when everything changed for me.

A mentor of mine once said: "If you knew you were going to make in profit $5 for every $1 you spent in marketing, how much would you spend on marketing?"

Your reaction might have been the same as mine when he asked me. I said, "I would put down at least $10,000 right now in marketing…" and he smiled and replied to me "Why wouldn't you put down every single dollar that you had access to? Loans, credit cards, savings…?"

I was a bit puzzled by his statement. But the point he was making was that I was just thinking way too small. If you already know something works, the only way to really cash in on it is to bet BIG!

If you're going to get back $5 for every $1…why not $20,000, or $50,000?

Thinking BIG has really changed my life! When I first started in direct mail marketing, I used to think spending $100 to just see what happens was the best way to do things.

In reality, direct mail marketing is a numbers game. If you want it to work in a really big way, then you need to have a bigger number of postcards mailed out, which equals a bigger number of sales, which equals a bigger number of back-end (secondary) sales...which equals a much larger amount of money in your pocket.

I understand this secret now.

And thinking big isn't just about marketing or advertising too. It's also one of the secrets of the top money earners in this industry. We'll talk about it later in another chapter...but let me just say this. You can't make millions of dollars in a $10 or $20 program. If you want to make really big money, you have to be in a program that allows you to get payments of $1,000, $5,000 or $9,000.

You don't see any lawyers, doctors, or rich investors talking about the sale or investment they made for $20! If you want to play the game like rich people, you have to talk and act like they do. You have to play for bigger amounts of money even if you feel like you're stretching your last dollar to make it happen...this is how people get really rich!

If you want to make $300 - $400 per month...no problem, join a $20 program. But **if you want to make $10,000, $20,000, $30,000 or more per month then keep reading as I show you how.**

Chapter 2

Learn First, Then Make Money

Chapter 2: Learn First, Then Make Money

Before you get too deep into learning about making money with direct mail marketing, it's important for you to know a few things up front about a direct mail marketing business.

It's really important that you know what you're doing and understand this industry. Direct mail marketing is like anything else in life. You don't try to fix your car or install a new shower in your home without first learning how to do it.

This is no different.

That's why the Mail Money Secrets program exists in the first place. There are thousands of people out there struggling to try to make a go of making money in direct mail marketing, with no clue what they're doing. I even know people that are trying to create their own direct mail marketing systems and programs and they've never actually made any money themselves. **This is very sad indeed.**

And it's no wonder that so many people are losing money in every single attempt.

Hopefully you found this book early on, before you spent too much money learning what "not to do" the hard way. And if you have already spent $1000's of dollars – consider this a fresh start for you, because now you'll be armed with the real knowledge and secrets that only the top experts know.

And better than that, you'll be able to implement everything by simply using the Mail Money Secrets system to start getting cash sent to your mailbox.

You don't have to worry about a big learning curve. You don't have to write sales copy, design postcards, or record sales pitches. Everything is already 100% done and proven to work already.

You just simply plug in.

I do want you to understand what is happening in the business and why I set it up this way, and that's why I wrote this book, so that you would fully understand the business while you are making big money in it.

The biggest misconception about direct mail marketing is that the top gurus are willing to share and teach you all of their secrets. While this might be true in other businesses, this is absolutely FALSE in direct mail marketing. Direct mail marketing gurus don't really want you to know how they actually make their money, because when there is more competition in the industry – there is frankly less money for them.

So why am I telling you this? Because it's time someone pulled the curtain back on this industry and started revealing the true secrets, the work it really takes and a step-by-step plan that you can follow to make real money from the comfort of your home simply mailing postcards or letters.

And in the spirit of full disclosure. I make money when you make money. So, if I give you the truth and show you how it's really done…you'll make more money AND so will I. That's how the Mail Money Secrets system works.

Like I said before, if you just want to make an extra $300 - $400 per month, this system is probably not for you.

But if you want to radically change your life and leave a legacy (and a fortune) for your kids and grandkids…then this system is exactly right for you. The sooner you get started and implement the marketing, the faster you'll see cash showing up in your mailbox like clockwork!

By the way, the best part about this business is that it's predictable. When I send out postcards, I get cash back in the mail…then I get bigger cash payments about 2 weeks later. Send more postcards, get more cash, then 2 weeks after, get more bigger cash payments.

If that sounds like something you would want…let's keep this going.

How to Make Millions in Direct Mail Marketing

Chapter 3

Building a
Customer List

Chapter 3: Building a Customer List

Did you ever buy a program through the mail and they told you that you could just mail a postcard, sales letter or offer and then watch the piles of cash, money orders or checks flood into your mailbox?

Of course, you have. We all have bought those things.

Here's the secret that all of those guru's don't want you to know. You are building a huge customer list for them to sell to over and over again. And they are doing it on the back of your dollar…not theirs!

So, what exactly should you be doing then if you can't afford to or don't know how to set up your own business?

You need to build a customer list and sell a high-priced back-end product to that customer list. (just like the gurus do).

Direct mail marketing isn't about the first sale. In the Mail Money Secrets system this is the first $100 that you will receive. It sounds great, but in reality, I just use that to buy more postcards (and you should too).

The real money is made when the back-end offer is made, and you get an express post-delivery from the USPS or FedEx that contains up to $9,000 in cash.

One customer. $9,000 in cash. How does that sound to you? That's a lot better than getting a lousy $20 in the mail or a commission check for $30, isn't it?

Consider this.

Most mail order programs, postcards, sales letters, affiliate offers actually LOSE MONEY when you mail them.

They also LOSE MONEY when the owner of the program mails them.

So, if everyone is losing money, how can they make a profit in direct mail marketing?

This is the secret about making a profit, but you MUST have this one already built into what you're doing, or it just won't work. It has to be automated for you.

It's called a High-Ticket Money Offer.

We will dig deeper into what this looks like in a direct mail marketing business, but for now, you must just understand that taking one small affiliate offer or one product for sale is NOT going to work by itself to make you money in direct mail marketing.

Your goal is only one thing when you send out a mailing and you're going to hate me for saying it. Because it's NOT to make money.

Your goal is to just build your initial customer list. Yes, you've probably heard it before but maybe you didn't really understand it.

When you send a mailing or a postcard to someone that has never purchased directly from you, all you are doing is SORTING OUT who is a buyer and who isn't a buyer. And you're just going to keep sending out new mailings and collecting this list of buyers over and over and over again…forever.

Next, once you have your list of buyers, you are going to make them a second offer. This offer is the thing that's going to bring you your BIG PROFITS.

These customers trust you and they have bought from you, so it's likely that they are going to buy again.

Remember, your profit in a mail order business is going to come from your 2nd sale to the same group of people that bought your first offer from you.

DON'T WORRY – IN THE MAIL MONEY SECERTS SYSTEM THE 2nd OFFER IS ALREADY <u>BUILT-IN AND 100% AUTOMATED FOR YOU</u>…SO YOU WON'T HAVE TO DO ANYTHING EXCEPT GET IT SET UP FOR YOURSELF.

Say this out loud:

"My big profits will NEVER be from the 1st sale."

It doesn't matter if you like this or not. Direct mail marketing doesn't care about your feelings. It doesn't care about how you wished it worked. It doesn't care about how you thought it worked.

It's just simple math.

> ***Send 1000 postcards to find 10 buyers.***
> ***You'll make a bit of money.***
> ***Then sell a bigger sale to those 10 buyers.***
> ***Then you get your BIG profits.***

Please don't overthink this part of direct mail marketing. And please don't think that some "GURU" has figured out how to get you big profits on your first mailing. It doesn't work that way and it will never work that way.

By the way, this was one of the hardest lessons I had to learn about direct mail marketing. Remember, when I told you that I went to a seminar and the expert there "fixed" what I was doing wrong. My 2nd sale is what he tweaked that resulted in my business exploding with profits over the months following. This is 100% essential to success and most direct mail marketing programs just mess it up.

So, let's see exactly what you need when you join a new direct mail marketing program or mail a postcard or sell something through the mail. This is non-negotiable.

You must have a good first sale that generates money and identifies your customers/buyers.

You must have a BIG second sale that automatically generates big profits.

There is no other way to operate.

Chapter 4
Selling to Your Customer List

Chapter 4: Selling to Your Customer List

You don't ever want to forget this one simple thing. Your customers are the GOLD in your business. So, if you treat them well, they will continue to buy from you over and over again. I've had customers that have been buying from me for over a decade and it's only because I deliver on what I promise.

Everything I promise to give them…is exactly what they receive. That makes happy customers and a constant flow of money into my bank account. And that's what you can get too once you start selling to your customer list.

But remember, step 1 is to build your customer list and this is going to cost a bit of money in advertising to do. It might cost of $1, $2, or even up to $5 per customer to build up your list. But once you have even just 10 or 20 customers on your list, you will be positioned to start making BIG PROFITS!

Do you know what the most frequently asked question that we get is? It's simply this: "When should I send the second offer to my customers?"

When? RIGHT NOW!

Once you have customers that are spending money with you, you'll want to immediately send them the next thing to buy.

You can make a good full time living or even a fortune with a really good 2nd offer.

Let's just assume that to find your customers, you sold them a small, low-ticket book, course, or system for somewhere between $40 - $100. This tends to be the range that most initial sales are made.

If you then have a $1,000, $5,000, or even $9,000 sale that you can make to those buyers, it will only take you just one 2nd sale to make all your money back from your mailings plus a nice profit.

If you don't have a high-ticket item to sell…you need to get one! You simply can't successfully operate a direct mail marketing business with just $10, $20, or $50 commissions. **You need to think in terms of $1,000's!**

My preference has always been to bump the sales into the thousands of dollars for the second sale because then I can get into a profit much quicker. For instance, the MMS Cash Club gives members a minimum payment of $1000 and all the way up to $9,000 for just 1 sale to 1 customer. That will pretty much put you into profit immediately.

Once you are getting big profits like $5,000 or $9,000 you can easily afford to really invest big in more marketing…which then just multiplies your results and sales so that you start earning $100,000's instead of just $1,000's.

Is this starting to make more sense to you then 99% of other direct mail marketing programs out there? I want to help you get rich…not just waste time in a hobby of doing mailings for tiny $10 payments.

Chapter 5
Multiple Streams
of Mail Income

Chapter 5: Multiple Streams of Mail Income

If you haven't yet figured it out, this is the most important part of mail order. Multiple streams simply mean that you have more than 1 thing to sell to customers.

Let me be clear though.

This <u>DOES NOT</u> mean joining 10 different programs and stuffing them all in an envelope to let your prospects choose one they like.

This <u>DOES NOT</u> mean joining every program that comes along so you can make 14 streams of income, $5 at a time.

This <u>DOES NOT</u> mean being in 7 different MLM programs because all of them might be the "next big thing" and you don't want to miss out.

Multiple streams of mail income are just 2 income streams combined into 1 simple program.

Multiple means more than one. It doesn't mean 17.

Multiple streams of mail income in the Mail Money Secrets program is the $100 that you receive from the 1st sale of the Mail Money Secrets system itself. Then the 2nd sale of the MMS Cash Club ($1,000 - $9,000). That's it.

You don't need to be in 17 different programs or have 12 income streams if your 2 income streams payout $100 and up to $9,000. In this case, two is really enough.

If you can make $9,000 per month from just getting one new customer…why would you ever waste your time being in mailing programs that sends you postage stamps, or $5, or a $25 commission?

Do you even know how many customers you would need at $5 to equal the same as one customer at $9,000?

Let me help you with the math. You would need 1,800 customers sending you $5. Who has the time or energy to chase around 1,800 people for $5? I am certainly not going to waste my time and I hope now that you see that you can get the same money from just one customer, you'll stop doing all of those ridiculous small dollar programs too.

By the way, this is the <u>number #1 reason why most people struggle and lose money in MLM/Network Marketing</u>. It's because are only making about $5 - 7 dollars per member in their downline.

So, you're going to stay away from small dollar programs and MLM programs. And that's why you are going to make **BIG PROFITS** in direct mail marketing. You are not restricted by someone else's rules. You are able to sell BIG TICKET sales to your customers. And you will.

Your direct mail marketing customers are going to want to buy things that will help them solve their problems. If you are selling a "make money" program or direct mail marketing business opportunity, then the best thing to sell to your customers is a business that's going to put cash directly into their pockets fast.

Like the Mail Money Secrets program.

That why, for instance, this book Mail Money Secrets is so popular. It offers an opportunity for people to resell it and make money…but at the same time teaches people about the **REAL SECRETS** of how to make money in the direct mail marketing industry.

The other thing that people LOVE in this industry is high-ticket/high-priced offers. There is nothing more enticing to your customers then the opportunity to earn a commission of $1,000, $5,000, or $9,000 dollars for just one sale.

High-Ticket sales are the fastest way to make a million dollars in mail order. Let's do the math and we'll show you why.

$20 commission sale = 50,000 customers = $1,000,000
$100 commission sale = 10,000 customers = $1,000,000
$1,000 commission sale = 1,000 customers = $1,000,000
$9,000 commission sale = 112 customers = $1,000,000+

And the question becomes. Do you think it's easier to find 50,000 customers or only 112 customers?

Considering that the acquisition of the customers in the first place is the most expensive part of the whole mail order business. If it costs you $5 in marketing to acquire a new customer – you would need to spend $250,000 to get 50,000 customers. But only $560 to get 112 customers.

And if you made $1,000,000+ would it be worth spending $560 to find them in the first place? Of course, it would.

This is why direct mail marketing works so well for those of us that understand the math. We are not trying to find 50,000 customers to send in $20. We are just trying to find 112 customers to send in $9,000!

And voila! You can be a direct mail marketing millionaire too!

Chapter 6
High Ticket
Mail Money

Chapter 6: High Ticket Mail Money

In the last chapter we showed you the simple math on why it makes more sense to sell a high-ticket item over lots of small priced items.

But the real problem isn't the math. The real problem is figuring out what to sell for thousands of dollars.

Here's the real trick that the gurus won't share with you. You need to have a product that has a retail value at or higher than the amount you are asking for.

If you don't have a real product that has a real value to the customer buying it, then you're just in a Ponzi scheme and someone is going to be going to jail. Trust me when I say no amount of money is worth risking going to jail. Not for me and not for you.

So, if you want to ask for $100, you'll need to sell something that is worth at least $100 or more. If you want to ask for $2,000, then you'll need to sell something that is worth $2,000 or more.

Unfortunately, this is just the way sales works. It's illegal to get people to pay you money for nothing. They have to get a real good value for their money! And if you are selling to people that want to make money like you do…they also need to be able to make a commission of $1,000 or $5,000 or $9,000 too!

If you can meet these requirements, then you have a homerun high-ticket sales offer and you'll be counting your $1,000,000 all the way to the bank!

In our first sale with the Mail Money Secrets system we always offer the Mail Money Secrets book and fully automated direct mail marketing postcard system. This gives incredible value to the customer in both information and in a fully automated, ready-to-take-orders business system.

In our second sale – the high-ticket mail money part of the Mail Money Secrets system – the MMS Cash Club, I fulfill the purchase with leads. So, you don't have to ever worry about shipping products or trying to come up with something worth $5,000 or $9,000 in value.

I take care of all of the fulfillment for you and I'll talk about that more as you read and listen to the overview of the system in the "Income Stream #2" part of the Mail Money Secrets book and system. The average person would not be able to provide such value to the customers, but I can because of my years of experience, my investments in lead systems, and success in this industry.

This way you can keep your $9,000 in cash that you'll be receiving from many people and leave 100% of the fulfillment to me. There won't be any measly 5% commissions with the Mail Money Secrets system. You'll keep 100% of the $9,000 for yourself!

Before we move on to the Income Streams part of this book and system, I'd like for you to just say this out loud. I know that you might think it's corny or weird, but I believe in the power of words and the power of speaking what you want. Here's what you need to say:

"I believe that I deserve to receive $9,000 cash payments in my mailbox, and I WILL receive $9,000 cash payments in my mailbox. I will do everything in my power to make this happen. I will not make excuses. I will not quit. I am believing with my heart and speaking with my mouth that $9,000 cash payments shall start coming into my mailbox and I am deserving of every dollar that I receive."

If you want to speed up the process, say this out loud every morning when you wake up and every night before you go to sleep.

It will become your reality and it will happen. (Also, you're going to take the action required in the "Income Streams" part of the book next to bring these cash payments into your life very fast.)

INCOME STREAM # 1

Mail Money Secrets System

How to Make Millions in Direct Mail Marketing

INCOME STREAM #1:
Mail Money Secrets System

24/7 RECORDED
FULL OVERVIEW OF
THE MAIL MONEY
SECRETS SYSTEM:

267-833-0592

(This is the original recording you listened to…you are ALREADY an active member in Income Stream #1)

The most difficult parts of direct mail marketing are:

1. Writing good sales copy/messaging
2. Having something good to sell

That's why I'm going to let you use the Mail Money Secrets System to sell. It's a completely 100% done-for-you direct mail marketing system. It's already setup, proven to work, and currently running, making me and others money through the mail.

The Mail Money Secrets System already has both the marketing material available for you and the information product deliverable (the book) done and ready for you to use.

STEP 1:
SEND THE MAIL MONEY
SECRETS POSTCARDS

STEP 2:
RECEIVE YOUR
$100 CASH ORDERS

STEP 3:
SEND US THE ORDERS WITH
$10 CASH TO COVER FULFILLMENT

Not only that, but we've also completely automated STEP 1 for you. So, you'll never have to label or stamp the postcards yourself. There are many programs out there that send you postcards to label and stamp.

(There is also an option for a do-it-yourself if you have your own leads or prefer to label, stamp and mail them yourself. I can print the full color postcards for you, and you can label, stamp and mail them yourself.)

Let's get real. I'm lazy and there's no way I'm going to do that work, so I'm not going to make you do it either!

Instead, just send me an order and I'll have the postcards custom printed (with your info on them), the leads printed on them and the postage printed on them. Then, the same company that does that for us will even take them over to the post office and drop them off.

This really limits the amount of driving around and wasting time to be successful. And when you get to know me better, you'll understand that we've got a lot of better things to do than put stamps on postcards…LIKE COUNT OUR CASH THAT COMES IN THE MAIL! Sound good?

So once the postcards are mailed out, the $100 cash orders are going to be sent directly to you. Just collect them daily or once a week, whatever works best for you, then mail the postcard with $10 over to us and we'll do all the fulfillment for you. We'll process the orders, keep track of you as the sponsor and send out the Mail Money Secrets System to your new customer.

Finally, once that's fulfilled, we are also going to make the INCOME STREAM #2 offer to your customers on your behalf. (Which you'll see in the next section). And this is where you'll make the really big money when you decide you want to participate.

By the way, when you purchased the Mail Money Secrets System for the $100 cash, you are fully qualified for your $100 cash payments to start coming directly to you.

Your next step is to join in on INCOME STREAM #2, then get some postcards mailed out and sit back and relax as the automated system takes care of the rest for you.

INCOME STREAM # 2

MMS
Cash Club

INCOME STREAM #2:
MMS CASH CLUB

24/7 RECORDED FULL OVERVIEW OF THE MMS CASH CLUB:

267-833-0592

THEN PRESS "27"

The original Mail Money Secrets recording will start to play, when the original recording starts, you will press "27" on your phone keypad to hear the **MMS CASH CLUB overview**

Please take a few minutes to listen to the full overview of the MMS Cash Club (Income Stream #2) now then go ahead and send us your registration and admin fees to get started.

I've also included a short list of frequently asked questions below for you to review after you've listened to the overview.

MMS CASH CLUB FAQ's

Question 1: Can I choose the smallest level now and upgrade later?

Answer 1: Yes, however you must pay the FULL amount of the level you wish to upgrade to. So, if you are at $1,000 and you want to upgrade to $3,000 level – you will pay the full $3,000 to upgrade, not just the difference. So, it's a much better deal to just start as close to the top or at the top. I recommend you start at the highest level that you can.

Question 2: Can I send a personal check or a money order?

Answer 2: No, cash only. That's why we call it a CASH CLUB. But remember that you only send this cash payment 1 time. You are then able to receive dozens or even hundreds of $1,000, $3,000, or even $9,000 cash payments in your mailbox. Would you rather get a personal check from someone (not sure if it will bounce) or would you rather just get cold, hard, spendable cash in the mail?

Question 3: Is it really safe to send $9,000 through the mail.

Answer 3: Yes, we've been accepting cash payments through the mail for years. And we recommend that you use a service like USPS Priority or Priority Express, or FedEx Express for delivery. That way, the cash is only in the mail for 1-2 days and its guaranteed delivery! (some people also mail their cash in a small book, magazine, or papers to "hide" it inside the express envelope.

Question 4: Will I get lots of cash payments to my mailbox?

Answer 4: I can't guarantee that you'll make a million dollars in cash using this system. No one can. But if you follow the system from start to finish. Register for the MMS Cash Club, then have us mail out postcards for you on a regular basis…the $100 orders can start really piling up for you and these are what turn in to the MMS Cash Club $1,000, $3,000 or even $9,000 cash orders through the mail. How many $9,000 cash payments would you like to receive each week?

Question 5: Is this really all I have to do? Register for the MMS Cash Club and then send the postcards?

Answer 5: Yes, that's it. Register for the MMS Cash Club, then send the postcards and we'll handle the rest for you.

Question 6: How many postcards should I start sending?

Answer 6: As many as you can. This system has already been fully tested and proven to convert and trust me when I say that it works like nothing you've ever seen before. This is the BEST marketing system ever created. (In my opinion).

Question 7: Can I start mailing postcards now and then upgrade in the MMS Cash Club later?

Answer 7: Yes, you can do that…but let me caution you that you'll be giving up a lot of dough if you do that. You'll miss out on all the orders for the MMS Cash Club that come in. I had a one lady join at the $1,000 level then mail out a bunch of postcards and she wasn't happy to find out that she missed out on 5 top level $9,000 orders – she only received $1,000 for each order for a total of $5,000 (she lost $8,000 per order). That mistake cost her $40,000 in cash.

Question 8: Should I wait until I can save up the $9,000 to join at the top level?

Answer 8: No, don't wait. You'll want to get started at the highest level you can immediately. Then start sending out postcards and re-invest what you can to grow. Sometimes it's the hard decisions and the risks that you take in life that really pay off the biggest. Imagine waking up to 3 MMS Cash Club payments next week for $9,000 each. That's $27,000 in cash. Or what about getting 10 MMS

Cash Club $9,000 payments in one month - $90,000 in cash. Would that change your life?

Question 9: Is there a product sold or delivered with the MMS Cash Club?

Answer 9: Yes, it's leads. But you don't have to worry about it. Once the cash payment to YOU is confirmed, we fulfill all of the orders with the full cash value in business opportunity leads.

PLEASE CHECK YOUR PACKAGE FOR INCOME STREAM #2 REGISTRATION INSTRUCTIONS.

Mail Money Secrets System Fulfillment

Fulfillment will be very easy for you since we are doing 100% of the fulfillment on your behalf.

You will receive 2 types of payments through the Mail Money Secrets System:

1. $100 CASH payments for the Mail Money Secrets System
2. $1,000, $3,000, $5,000, $7,000, or $9,000 payments for the MMS Cash Club.

In both cases we just ask that you send us the information for the order and we'll do all of the fulfilment for you.

$100 MAIL MONEY SECRETS SYSTEM ORDER:

Please send us the following:

1. $10 CASH payment for fulfillment
2. The original postcard with your name and the new member's name on it.

Note: if you don't have the original postcard to send to us, please send us your name and address, AND send in your new member's name and address AND include a note that this is for the MAIL MONEY SECRETS SYSTEM.

We will fulfill the Mail Money Secrets system with this book and the forms for them to join the MMS Cash Club.

MMS CASH CLUB ORDERS:

In most cases we will already know the new member's information for the MMS Cash Club since they will also be sending us a $100 Administration fee directly.

Please send us the following:

1. No payment **(you keep 100% of your CASH)**
2. The original registration form for the MMS Cash Club

Note: if you don't have the original form to send to us, please send us your name and address, AND send in your new member's name and address AND include a note that this is for the MMS Cash Club and the amount of CASH that they sent to you.

We will fulfill the MMS Cash Club with their leads and welcome package for the MMS Cash Club.

EARNINGS DISCLAIMER

MAIL MONEY SECRETS IS A BOOK THAT SHOWS HOW TO MAKE MONEY IN DIRECT MAIL MARKETING BUSINESSES.

ALL EARNINGS OR INCOME STATEMENTS BY OUR COMPANY AND ANY OF OUR AFFILIATE MEMBERS ON OUR WEBSITES, SALES LETTERS, BOOKS, POSTCARDS, OR ANY OTHER MATERIAL NOT OWNED BY US BUT REFERRING TO OUR BUSINESS ARE ONLY ESTIMATES OR EXAMPLES OF WHAT IS POSSIBLE AND WHAT SOME PEOPLE HAVE EARNED. THERE IS NO ASSURANCE OR GUARANTEE THAT YOU'LL EARN A SIMILAR INCOME, OR THAT YOU WILL EARN ANY INCOME AT ALL.

EARNINGS AND INCOME EARNED THROUGH USING OUR COMPANY'S METHODS AND SERVICES ARE STILL 100% BASED ON YOUR EFFORTS TO BUILD YOUR OWN BUSINESS SUCCESS.

WE DO NOT TAKE RESPONSIBILITY FOR YOUR SUCCESS OR FAILURE BY USING ANY OF OUR BOOKS, PRODUCTS, SERVICES, WEBSITES, OR SYSTEMS. ANY AND ALL CLAIMS, REPRESENTATIONS, TESTIMONIALS OR INCOME OR RESULTS USING OUR BOOKS, PRODUCTS, SERVICES, WEBSITES, OR SYSTEMS ARE NOT TO BE CONSIDERED AS AVERAGE RESULTS. OUR TESTIMONIALS COME FROM A WIDE RANGE OF MEMBERS FROM BEGINNERS TO TOP EARNERS AND WE CANNOT GUARANTEE YOU WILL GET SIMILAR RESULTS BY FOLLOWING THE SAME BUSINESS MODEL THEY ARE USING.

WE REPRESENT THE POTENTIAL OF OUR BUSINESS TO THE BEST OF OUR ABILITY BASED ON OUR SUCCESS USING THE METHODOLOGIES THAT WE TEACH AND THE MATERIALS THAT WE SELL. HOWEVER, THERE CAN BE NO ASSURANCE THAT ANY PRIOR SUCCESS, PAST RESULTS, OR SUCCESS OF OTHER PEOPLE WILL TRANSLATE TO INCOME OR SUCCESS FOR YOU. THERE IS NO ASSURANCE THAT ANY PAST SUCCESS CAN BE USED TO INDICATE ANY FUTURE INCOME OR RESULTS WITH OUR METHODS.

YOUR INCOME RESULTS ARE FIRST AND FOREMOST BASED ON YOU. WE HAVE NO WAY TO PREDICT YOUR RESULTS WITH YOUR BUSINESS SINCE WE DO NOT KNOW YOU, YOUR BACKGROUND, YOUR BUSINESS

ACUMEN, WORK ETHICS OR ANY OTHER FACTOR THAT CONTRIBUTES TO SUCCESS IN YOUR OWN PERSONAL BUSINESS.

WE DO NOT GUARANTEE OR IMPLY THAT YOU WILL GET RICH, BE ABLE TO QUIT YOUR JOB, OR MAKE ANY MONEY AT ALL. THERE IS NO GUARANTEE THAT YOU WILL GET THE SAME RESULTS OF OTHER PEOPLE USING THE SAME BUSINESS MODEL AND MATERIALS. HOME BASED BUSINESSES AND ONLINE BUSINESSES HAVE UNKNOWN RISKS AND ARE NOT SUITABLE FOR EVERYONE.

YOU SHOULD MAKE YOUR OWN PERSONAL DECISION IF THIS IS RIGHT FOR YOU BEFORE STARTING OR JOINING THIS OR ANY BUSINESS ONLINE. YOU ARE FULLY RESPONSIBLE FOR YOUR OWN DECISION TO JOIN THIS OR ANY RELATED BUSINESS AND WE DO NOT ACCEPT ANY RESPONSIBILITY FOR YOUR SUCCESS OR FAILURE BY ENGAGING OUR COMPANY'S PRODUCTS AND SERVICES.

Made in the USA
Middletown, DE
22 June 2023

32943446R00035